Class of '54:
Memoirs
of a
Yale Man

By

Dr. David William Foerster

HAWK Publishing Group
www.hawkpub.com

LIBRARY OF CONGRESS CATALOG IN PUBLICATION DATA

Class of '54: Memoirs of a Yale Man /David William Foerster

[1. Foerster, David William-Autobiography-United States.
2. United States-Memoirs.]

Library of Congress Control Number: 2004109075
Published in the United States by HAWK Publishing Group.
Cover photo courtesy of www.freestockphotos.com.

HAWK Publishing Group
7107 South Yale Avenue #345
Tulsa, OK 74136
918-492-3677
www.hawkpub.com

HAWK and colophon are trademarks belonging to the
HAWK Publishing Group.

Printed in the United States of America.
9 8 7 6 5 4 3 2 1

Class of '54:
Memoirs
of a
Yale Man

By
Dr. David William Foerster

Dedication

This story is dedicated to the men, living and dead, of the Yale University Class of '54. While some became famous, such as Bill Wrigley and Howard Johnson, most of us did not.

Foreword

There are many serious pitfalls in writing a memoir. Since most of our lives are somewhat mundane, it might be deemed arrogant to assume that what I have to relate is worthy of a reader's time or interest. Therefore, I have woven my memories with a clever sleight of hand—changing names and places when necessary to ensure the adventures I depict are a microcosm of the mores, the sensuality, and the aspirations of all young men of the almost forgotten decade of the 1950s. I hope that you will feel the difference of this era, since it bears little resemblance to the sexual revolution of the '60s and '70s, the "me first" feelings of the '80s or the internationalism of the '90s into the 21st century.

The '50s were a simpler time. With the Korean War in the past and Vietnam on the horizon, there was time for young men and women to reflect and prepare for their futures. Alcohol was the primary recreational drug, and the distant rumblings of Communism seemed worlds away. There was no urgency, no overwhelming pressure—it was truly a time to be treasured.

Although it is tempting to embellish everyday events, to promote self-aggrandizement, to enhance one's prowess with the opposite sex, to exhibit great wisdom in solving complex problems that might arise, and to exaggerate physical skills, giving in to such temptations would defeat the primary purpose of the memoir: to accurately convey the atmosphere and uniqueness of the times. Of course, such false ingredients would add flavor and spice to the stew, but they would also taint the meat. On the other hand, the use of different names and a small degree of literary license has allowed me to smooth the flow of events and polish any rough edges.

Please note that I never intended to embarrass or demean; my goal was simply to enlighten others about a fascinating, surprising, delightful time in my life. Simply enjoy the story as it unfolds, as I believe it will be different than you think!

Dr. David William Foerster

PART ONE: THE IDEA

As the Blackbird in the spring,
'neath the willow tree.
Sat and piped, I heard him sing:
sing of Aura Lee,
Aura Lee, Aura Lee,
maid with golden hair.
Sunshine came along with thee,
and swallows in the air.

Refrain from *Aura Lee*
By George Poulton & W.W. Fosdick

The Beginning

I'm not really sure how the idea originated. Maybe it was something I saw or read or perhaps it was simply an unrealistic wild notion, but early in the fall of my senior year at Yale, I developed an obsession: I would travel to Europe after graduation in June and return before the first day of Med school in September. Every summer for three years I had cleaned, stacked and loaded cast concrete sills and coping at the Harding Stone Company. Since it was hard, repetitive work, I was always more than ready to return to school each fall. With only nine months of undergraduate classes to tackle, I yearned for a change of pace and a release from such intense physical labor. Even with three-fourths of a year to bring my desire to fruition, I knew it would take every day to plan, scheme and develop such a major undertaking.

My first challenge was to sell the idea to my father, since his financial backing was an absolute necessity. A self-made, hard working man, he rarely spent a dime on foolishness. Although he could afford to drive a Lincoln or Cadillac, he preferred a Ford or a Chevy so that he could invest the savings in stocks or bonds. When my acceptance to Yale arrived, he was so proud that he freely agreed to pay my expenses, and in a moment of weakness, he even offered to buy me a new car (certainly a Ford or Chevy) upon graduation.

I knew that if I could convince him to postpone the new car until I graduated from Med school, then he would not have to spend so much money in the spring of '54 and maybe, just maybe, I could convince him to spend a little on my trip to Europe. It would be imperative that such a trip be the world's greatest bargain, so I was certain I had to carefully weigh and calculate every detail before broaching the subject. I set my sights on finding a bottom dollar deal by Christmas break so I could successfully present my case.

When it came to spending money, my father did have a small, but susceptible, Achilles' heel. He derived great happiness from traveling and spent as much as necessary to enjoy the places he visited. I knew that if I could arouse his passion for adventure, it would greatly enhance my chance for success. So, in the fall of '53 I began to seek the ways and means to accomplish my dream.

Junior Year

At the start of my junior year, I would have never had the time or inclination to pursue such an elaborate plan. Since I had saved $200 while working at Harding over the summer, in early October, my good friend Daniel and I pooled our funds to buy a nice, mechanically sound, 1950 two-door Buick sedan from a used car dealer in New Haven.

Because the Yale campus was located on the edge of downtown New Haven, there were no parking lots for students and most of the streets had parking meters. However, there was an uphill street on the back part of campus that led to the Chemistry Lab. It had buildings on one side, large trees lining a cemetery on the other, and no meters. Daniel and I figured the trees offered a little protection from the sun and elements, so we decided to park there like many other students.

Because New Haven is on the ocean (Long Island

Sound) it seldom got as much snow and cold weather as inland New England. Instead, dreary clouds and frozen rain occasionally marked the fall and winter months.

About a week after we bought the Buick, a typical cold rain abruptly turned to sleet. In a matter of minutes, ice coated everything and the streets and sidewalks became dangerously slick. All morning I kept hearing about the tree limbs that had broken from the weight of the ice and how one huge branch had fallen on a car parked near the Chemistry Lab. During a break between classes, I decided that it might be a good idea to check our car to make sure it was okay.

As I approached the fateful parking place, I spotted a small crowd gawking at the giant limb that had pleated the roof of the car. I instantly realized it was our poor Buick! Although the Street Department had cut off the portion blocking traffic, the remaining stump was still leaning against the car like a drunken sentry.

Son of a bitch! I silently screamed as I shoved the huge, tipsy intruder off the car. The roof pleat extended across the front passenger side including the window frame. The window glass of the door was shattered, but intact. I managed to unlock and open the front door and even rolled down the glass. Daniel soon joined me and we cursed our bad luck.

Since he was an engineering major, he thought that the two of us could lie on the front seat, put our feet on the roof and push with all our young athletic ability until the roof regained its former shape. First, however, we put the bumper jack into the window frame to expand both the frame and roof edge. Then with sheer leg power, we managed to push up the roof enough for a passenger to sit comfortably without hitting his or her head. By screwing around with the bumper jack, we even managed to get the window to roll up and down. So, the elements be damned, we were back in business!

Moreover, when it rained later that day, we had the only car in New Haven with a permanent birdbath on the roof. *C'est la vie!*

Daniel was dating Essie, a girl from Conn College, which was the popular term for the Connecticut College for Women in New London, Connecticut. Since it was about sixty miles from New Haven, he had used the Buick for many of his sojourns. In spite of the Buick's resemblance to a WWII tank, it still provided a fine method of transportation.

After a short time, Essie decided that I would make a perfect blind date for her roommate, Norma. Since I wasn't going with anyone at the time and there was a big home football game that weekend, I agreed. Daniel and I arranged for the girls to stay at a local hotel and we met their train when it rolled into New Haven on Friday evening. Norma was an attractive, medium height brunette with a pleasant smile and voice. The moment I laid eyes on her I couldn't have been more delighted! In spite of her layered clothing and winter coat, it was obvious that she was slender. Even though Essie had promised Daniel that she was cute, I was well aware of the tendency of girls to see things in each other that guys found perplexing. I was relieved and intrigued, since I'd been worried that she might be fat and homely!

In fact, Norma and I got along so well that the evening ended with some nice good-night kisses before we left the girls at the hotel. Saturday we went to the game, did a little drinking and screamed *Go Bulldogs!* until the flask went dry. After the game, Daniel suggested that I show Norma my apartment and then meet the two of them later for dinner. Since it sounded like a good idea, Norma and I headed for my place at Berkley College.

Yale had a unique living arrangement for its 3,000 or so upperclassmen. There were ten large apartment quadrangles called "residential colleges" that each housed approximately 300 males. Every unit had a dining hall, a library, and several meeting rooms. The apartment-like suites on each floor typically accommodated four students. In addition, every college housed a residential "Master," usually a prominent professor, who had a sizable apartment with several guest rooms. Although his job was mostly ceremonial, he was in charge of any problems that occurred on the premises.

I shared a suite of rooms with three close friends. We had a large living area with a fireplace filled with hundreds of neatly bent beer cans, walls that we had painted forest green, and well-worn sofas and chairs. The old rug that covered the floor had actually been swept within the past week. A short hall led to a middle bedroom that Al and Ron shared, and the back bedroom where Paul and I lived. Bunk beds, dressers and desks were the bedroom's only furnishings. We lived on the second floor, sharing a stairway with a similar suite across the hall, as well as two above and two on the ground level. Each floor had a single large bath with several sinks, showers and toilets.

There was only one rule at Yale concerning the residential colleges and it was enforced by a penalty of expulsion: No women were allowed to spend the night. Aside from the obvious moral issues, this allowed residents the freedom to take a leak and shower in the morning without having to worry about running into someone's girlfriend. If any other rules existed, they were routinely ignored, leaving us free to come and go with whomever we pleased during the day and evening.

As we entered the living room, I knew that all my roommates were gone for the weekend. Al and Ron had left to visit Smith, an exclusive female college in Massachusetts, and Paul was in New York City with friends. After the usual pleasantries, I decided to create the perfect atmosphere by turning on the record player. Norma and I sat on the couch, talking for a while until we began enjoying a little smooching. It was obvious that she liked me and I felt something for her as well.

When I offered to show her the rest of the suite, she was more than agreeable. Soon we were stretched on the lower bunk bed doing some serious kissing and petting. I unbuttoned the top three buttons on her blouse and slid my hand over her bra-covered breasts. She was neither big nor small, probably a B cup and it felt wonderful to touch her warm, soft breast. Better yet, she did not attempt to push my hand away. I gently rolled her toward me, reached around and unhooked her bra. Feeling her soft breast beneath her bra really awakened my manhood and soon my hand was moving down her thighs. Again, very gently I raised her skirt and used my hand to explore her inner thighs. She had on a panty girdle and much

10

to my surprise and joy there was a small tear in the crotch that allowed my exploring finger to enter that wonderfully wet opening of her womanhood.

What happened in the next few moments I am not sure, but soon I was standing by my dresser, stripping off my pants as I searched for the three pack Trojans that I'd been saving for an eternity in the back of the top drawer. I pulled off the wrapper and began unrolling the latex sheath over my very firm and eager organ. I never did understand why they made the damn things so long—maybe the ring remaining at the base acted as a French tickler—who knows?

Norma had removed her skirt and panty girdle while I was doing my rubber act. She still had on her blouse and unfastened bra and I had on my half unbuttoned shirt but who cared! I slipped in between her spread legs and in the finest missionary fashion we pumped our heaving groins until the Nirvana of orgasm pulsed through our bodies.

Afterward we carefully dressed, went back to the living room and talked for a long time. She freely told me I was the third person with whom she had made love. Her first time was during her senior year in high school with her steady boyfriend. Number two was a summer romance between her freshman and sophomore years and I was number three. This didn't bother me since I had had five previous experiences (which I didn't share with her). Two were with wild girls and the other three with prostitutes. Norma was my first time with what most people would consider a "decent" girl, although I had been orgasmic with my high school sweetheart as well as with a few other girls during heavy petting and fully clothed friction. Fear of pregnancy with its social disgrace made most girls very careful. The only form of birth control was "rubbers" (latex condoms). Since abortion was unlawful and confined to back alleys with horror tales of infection and death, it was up to the man to protect the girl he cared for by abstaining from vaginal sex as long as possible in the relationship. If marriage was imminent, then sex with rubbers was okay. Not all guys followed this creed, but it was more common than not during the '50s. Occasionally a girl that who slipped in high school would become "revirginized" in college when it was time to find a husband. At the time, I was glad that Norma was honest and didn't pull the "first time" bullshit on me.

After Daniel and I put the girls on the train Sunday morning, he began to quiz me about Norma. How well did we get along? Did I like her? Was I going to keep seeing her? He seemed quite pleased when I told him we had gotten along fine and were going to keep seeing each other. He then turned serious and asked if I could keep a secret. I said "of course," so he confessed that he and Essie were having sex. Although I wanted to tell him about Norma and me, I didn't.

12

Within a few days, however, Norma told Essie and Essie told Daniel, so the four of us shared the personal secret. I never told Paul, Ron or Al, but as time passed, I'm sure they figured it out.

Daniel and I spent a lot of time going to New London in the hard time Buick. At first we argued about who had to drive but eventually took turns. The bench front seat was longer than the rear seat and was roomier even though the steering wheel took up a little space. The girls had become quite comfortable having sex in the presence of the other couple who were basically out of view because of the seat back. Our usual modus operandi was to take the girls to dinner and a movie, then park and steam up the car. The girls had to be in by midnight so Daniel and I usually arrived back in New Haven by 1:30 a.m.

All was, however, not rosy and delicious. I received an allowance of $50 per month which was gone within the first two weeks. Daniel received a great deal more money than I did, but I didn't feel right asking him to pay my share, too. Finally, I told Norma that as much as I wanted to see her every weekend, I just didn't have the money.

She was very understanding and came up with a novel idea. Her father was a highly successful industrialist in upstate New York, so it would be no problem for her to supply me an additional allowance of $50 for the final two weeks of the month. No one had to know of our arrangement, not even Essie and Daniel. I would simply have money in my pocket to pay our way. Oh, my God! What a deal. Money, sex and rubbers!

Unfortunately, the hard time Buick began breaking down on a regular basis and quickly turned into a one-way slot machine. Norma frequently helped pay Daniel for my half of the repairs. Over the winter and spring, we replaced every electrical and hydraulic piece that could possibly fail. Late one Sunday night near Old Lyme, the points (ignition) broke, leaving Daniel and I stranded in the bitter cold of a New England winter night.

No one stopped to pick us up. Furthermore, it became much too cold to stand in the freezing wind while trying to thumb a ride. So we got back into the car, wrapped two blankets around us (which fortunately were in the trunk) and spent the night huddled together in spoon fashion trying to beat the cold. Every 30 minutes or so one of us would say "shift" and we would reverse the spoon. Finally, daylight crept over the frigid highway and a kind soul stopped to give us passage to New Haven.

Daniel arranged to have the car towed into Old Lyme and have the points replaced. A few days later, we found a ride to the repair shop and brought Hard

Times back home. Later we were able to laugh about our misadventures and tease the girls about the night we "slept together" without them!

As the four of us became closer, we also became bolder. One afternoon at Daniel's apartment, we decided to adjourn to his bedroom for some extra-curricular activities. Daniel and I pushed his desk against the door since there was no way to lock it. Daniel and Essie crawled up into the upper bunk, while Norma and I chose the lower. Soon clothes were strewn all over the floor and the bunk bed was rocking. Suddenly the door smashed into the desk when Daniel's roommate tried to get in. With cat-like reflexes, I shot out of bed and slammed the barely open door shut, screaming to the would-be intruder to come back later.

As I turned around there were six eyes staring at me as round as hoot owls, connected to three totally naked bodies all sitting upright in total shock. I hadn't realized Essie had such nice boobs since until that moment I had never seen her stripped bare. On a few occasions, Norma and I had peeked into the front seat of the Buick and giggled silently while watching Daniel's bare butt pumping between Essie's elevated knees. No real frontal nudity was visible then, so it was a surprise to see so much of her bare skin. The glimpse, however, was quite brief as I sprung quickly back into Norma's arms—and other areas. Soon the bunk bed was bouncing as if nothing had happened. I never heard what Daniel's roomie had to say and never really cared. Years later Daniel and I wondered why we didn't work out a girlfriend swap, but at that time, such an idea never remotely occurred to us.

All too soon, spring was gone and it was time to return home for the summer. We said our good-byes to the girls, promised to write often and sold the ratty Buick to a fellow student for $100. Later he told us it ran perfectly for the next year, no doubt due to all the parts that we had replaced. Daniel and I debated about storing it for the summer but this was not feasible and we were delighted to unload it. There was no way we would have driven it home to Oklahoma.

I suppose I knew all along that I wasn't in love with Norma. As the summer stretched out, I wrote her less and less. It wasn't that I didn't care about her, I really did and I would have fought anyone to protect her if necessary. But, and this was a big but, she was not the one. I simply couldn't imagine spending the rest of my life with her.

Finally, I wrote the big nasty, saying I had met a hometown girl and had fallen for her. None of this really happened but I felt it was the easiest way to break up. Norma wrote back a seething letter about what a rotten person I was and if that was what I wanted it was fine with her. I knew, however, that she was deeply hurt and I felt like a real bastard. I told Daniel what I had done and sensed that he too was becoming cool toward Essie. Soon after returning to Yale for the fall semester, Daniel and Essie broke up, too.

As time passed, my social life seemed depressing without Norma. In a weak moment, I called her. Somehow, I convinced her to join me for the big football game that weekend. There was a distant coldness in her voice but my hormones overrode all common sense and I visualized her succumbing to my charms at least one more time. How wrong I was! Norma was pleasant, but cool, and refused even a nuance of romance. A few hugs, a couple of short kisses, nothing more. Sunday morning when I put her on the train to New London, I knew it was our last goodbye. I never saw Norma again.

PART TWO: THE FRUITION

*The '50s resonated with both
the beauty and the meaning
of Doris Day's famous song -
Que Sera Sera!*

19

Senior Year

As I began talking to my roommates and friends about how much I wanted to go to Europe, a certain communications aura was created that floated beyond my circle of acquaintances. As if ordained by a mystic force I soon gained knowledge of a 2nd year student who had similar interests. Friends of friends introduced us.

Thomas was a sophomore from a prominent New York family, and was pleasant, easy going and friendly. We hit it off instantly and were soon in serious conversation about going to Europe. We found we had much in common including football. Thomas was a reserve fullback on the Yale Varsity and I was the fullback for the Berkley College team. I had always wanted to play football, but never felt I had the speed or strength while in high school.

When I entered Yale, I was 5'8", weighed 165 pounds, and was only 16 years old. Thanks to heredity,

Harding Stone Company and sheer luck, I was 185 pounds and 6' by the time I started my junior year. By today's standards, I probably would have been considered a "hunk," but in the '50s it didn't seem important to girls. What was most important was how one appeared socially.

We had a word for the quality of being smooth, cool, aristocratic and suave: "shoe." The word was derived from the dirty, charcoal gray bucks worn by the really cool guys. Bucks were white leather shoes with red rubber soles. Since the leather had a slight but definite fuzzy surface, they were impossible to polish. There was nothing more "unshoe" than neat, clean white bucks. It took a great deal of time and wear for the bucks to take on the desired dingy gray shade, although we found that by rubbing charcoal on the surface we could rapidly speed the process!

I suppose the shoes were a microcosm of the elite status. Just as the aristocracy of the eastern preppies required a long line of "noble" ancestors, so the shoes required a great deal of time to acquire the proper patina. Dirty bucks, khaki pants, an old tweed sports coat with a button down shirt, and a tie with small narrow stripes was the proper uniform of a shoe collegian.

Since it took considerable time and dedication to play Varsity football at Yale, there were a great number of former high school players available to play residential college football. With 300 men in each college, it was easy to assemble 25 or 30 good players. Since there were 10 colleges, we had a solid nine game season.

Other residential college sports were also available, including soccer, crew, basketball, squash, tennis, swimming and baseball. At the end of the year, they tallied all the results using a formula (with football carrying the most weight) and the winning college received a large trophy that carried a great deal of prestige.

During my junior year, all three of my roommates tried out for football and became the starting halfbacks and the end. They urged me to try out, too, but since I hadn't played in high school, I reluctantly passed. About three games into the season, the starting fullback hurt his shoulder and had to quit. At the pleadings of my roomies, I filled the opening and became the team's fullback. Having played lacrosse on the freshman and junior varsity teams, I was reasonably tough. I learned quickly and actually had a great deal of success. In fact, during my senior year I was the leading scorer in the league and made the All-Star team as a fullback.

So, when I met Thomas, we had an instant bond as football fullbacks. Thomas was 6'1" and weighed about 200 pounds. His blondish hair and blue eyes made him attractive to the "fairer sex," which is now a politically incorrect term meaning women. Thomas had already done a great deal of research on European trips and had found that the Holland-American Lines had regular student sailings throughout the summer. The cost was approximately $400 round trip, which was a great deal. Thomas had already made his reservation and had a commitment from Harris, a former prep friend at Vanderbilt, but they really wanted a third person to share expenses. Since Thomas had the right contacts, they planned to rent a car in Paris and spend two months motoring through Central Europe. A third person to split expenses would benefit everyone, so I was invited to join the fun.

Of course, I still had to convince my father of the trip's benefits so he would provide the financing. Thomas had figured that the three of us could cover the cost of gas, inexpensive meals and cheap hotels on $10 per day per person. My share of the car rental was $100, so I needed $700 cash, a $400 ticket for the ship and a round trip train ticket from Oklahoma to NYC. Since a new car could run over $2000, I hoped for the best.

To lay a strong foundation, I began dropping little hints in my letters home. I suggested that it might be time to spend my summer doing something that had cultural and educational benefits. I reminded my parents that Med school was a long, hard grind and because of my good grades and academic achievement, perhaps I deserved a little reward. . .

When I arrived home for the Christmas Holidays (the old term for today's "mid-winter break") I began gradually working on my father. I told him about Thomas's plans for a wonderful, yet inexpensive, trip to Europe. I suggested that Thomas was begging me to join him, but that I knew it was my father's decision, not mine. I explained that the trip was what I wanted to do most in my life, and that I would be willing to give up the new car to go. (Well, maybe not totally give it up, rather postpone it until Med school graduation.)

I also knew that my father was planning to buy a '54 Chevy coupe in the fall and that I might be able to have his old '50 model. He seemed receptive and said he needed a little time to think. I also asked my mother to help, since she was almost always on my side. She agreed and the subject silently loomed until a few days before I returned to Yale.

Finally, after months of planning and plotting my father fulfilled my dreams! He generously agreed to postpone the new car, and finance the trip. *Joy to the World!* never sounded so good, and I was on cloud nine when I arrived in New Haven. I quickly called Thomas, told him I was in, and that we would soon find ourselves in the Promised Land.

Thomas and I had several meetings over the next few months, making sure deposits were sent in a timely fashion and planning our itinerary. One of the requirements for sailing was a mandatory Holland American sponsored student tour. We picked the shortest (and cheapest), a two day tour of Amsterdam with a one day bike tour of the countryside. We would then be free to pick up our car in Paris and explore on our own until it was time to return.

The second semester of my senior year was great. I only had to take three classes, so I had free time to write my thesis and do the required reading for comprehensive testing in my major—Human Evolution and Culture. I was excused from all finals, so I only had to take my comprehensive exam, which was not very difficult. I wrote my thesis on the social and cultural mechanisms of group acceptance, using my experience at Harding Stone Company as relevant material.

Since finals week was in early May, I had time to go home and spend three weeks with my family before returning for graduation on June 1. This also gave me a chance to round up the things I needed for the trip. Although I didn't smoke, we had heard that American cigarettes were highly prized by Europeans, so I packed three cartons to use for tips. I also bought some quick drying socks and underwear, a cheap camera, and plenty of film.

My father had never said much to me about sexual behavior and morals, but before I left he quietly confided that I should be sure to use a rubber if the situation presented itself in Europe. Of course, he was fully aware that I planned to try out some European stuff. Therefore, two dozen Trojans were included in the trip necessities, which turned out to be a bit optimistic!

We took a family motor trip in my mother's Packard sedan to New Haven for graduation, returning through Michigan where my father was born. His father was a first generation German-American and when he married my grandmother, who was born in Hamburg, their only offspring, my father, was a full blood German-American. Since my mother was a mixture of English, Scotch, and a little German, I was born a true mixed cultural American. I have never understood why so many people, especially those in the media, refer to "Latino-Americans," "African-Americans," etc. We are all Americans and should simply be called "Americans." How many of us are pure stock of any race or culture? Darned few, I'd wager.

The student sailing was in the middle of June, which gave me time to reorganize and pack before catching a train to New York City. Thomas and his mother met me at Grand Central Station and took me to their home about 35 miles north and east of the

Big Apple. It was very nice and they were obviously a family of means. Late the next morning we loaded our luggage and Thomas's mother drove us to the Holland American pier. Harris arrived from Tennessee with his parents and we all exchanged pleasantries. Harris was shorter than Thomas, but was solidly built with blond hair and hazel eyes. He was captain of Vanderbilt's wrestling team and was definitely a stud.

It was on the pier that we got the first look at the S.S. Zeiderkris. She was a medium size vessel that had been converted from a WWII troop carrying "Liberty" ship, into a civilian passenger liner specially equipped for student sailings. Staterooms held six people with males and females segregated by decks. We learned that our ship had booked approximately 700 females and only 140 males when we arrived. This was very exciting news, but as we scanned the milling crowd, it became apparent that of the 700, only about 50 could be called "lookers." I wasn't worried; however, since I figured three good looking guys who were really shoe would do alright. In some ways, I was right, but not altogether.

As we boarded the ship in the early afternoon, I spotted a cute, sharply dressed girl of medium height with blondish hair at a distance. She was too far away to start a conversation, but I made a mental point to find her later and get acquainted. Something about her was intriguing. She was definitely *shoe*.

PART THREE: THE VOYAGE

Anchors Aweigh, my boys,
Anchors Aweigh!
Farewell to college joys,
we sail at break of day-ay-ay-ay.

Refrain from the
US Navy Theme Song

Setting Sail

The ship was far more comfortable than I expected. Although mainly Indonesian with Dutch officers, virtually all of the crew spoke excellent English. Thomas, Harris, and I were assigned to a cabin with two other guys, Ray and Bob. They were both Jewish, very nice and a little shoe. There were no locks on any of the cabin doors, but we were assigned small lockers where we could keep our valuables, passports, money, etc. I suppose the *no lock* policy was to minimize private areas and thus prevent any hanky panky or serious make-outs in the cabins. In fact, there was no place on deck or elsewhere to be alone with a girl. Such a bummer!

Shortly after we began our voyage, Thomas, Harris and I agreed to sample a woman in every country we visited. We discussed the problem communication would undoubtedly create, and decided that our amorous adventures might require the services of ladies of the night. Since we were heavily stocked with rubbers, and penicillin, the wonder drug, had all but eliminated venereal diseases, we toasted to our impending sexual endeavors.

We spent the first evening meeting people and visiting. The ship had a nice nightclub where a student band played all evening. Although the three of us met many people, both male and female, I never saw the girl who caught my eye on the pier. She apparently was not socializing. (I found out why later.)

Rough seas the next day made many kids seasick. I felt a little queasy myself, but still managed to get around. Of course, fewer people made it easier to have more long and meaningful conversations. Sharon was one of the lucky few who didn't get sick. I met her that afternoon and we talked for a long time.

Although she was not the mysterious girl on the pier, she was nice looking, dark complected, and from the Midwest. We made a date for that evening to meet at the nightclub for a beer and dancing. One of the really great things about the ship was the beer! Wonderful, full-bodied beer from Holland in green bottles and, oh my goodness, so cheap to buy: nine cents in American money. With a ten percent tip (one cent), one thin dime went a long way!

I introduced Sharon to Thomas and Harris who were finally getting their sea legs, so they joined us for a few beers. After some dancing, I invited Sharon for a walk around the ship in hopes of finding somewhere to make out, since she seemed interested. Unfortunately, we found no convenient place and had to settle for a few good night kisses and nothing more. She was an eager, good kisser, and even though I liked her, there really weren't any strong feelings developing.

After leaving her with her roommates, I returned to my cabin where Thomas and Harris eagerly awaited news of the big event. There was, of course, not much to tell, and I said I probably wasn't going to date her anymore. This seemed to rev them up, since it was obvious they both liked what they had seen. So, I basically said, "more power to you."

I'm not sure if either of them really did all that well with her, but she remained a good friend and frequently washed my dirty clothes during the rest of the journey. I really appreciated this, as I had never done any laundry. I hadn't led a sheltered life, but my mother had always done the laundry at home, as had the school laundry at Yale.

The next day was much smoother and more people were roaming the decks. I spent the afternoon sunning and playing bridge. The girl on the pier had yet to surface, but I kept looking.

The big event for the evening was a current American

movie. After dinner I asked Thomas and Harris to save me a place while I ran back to the cabin for a sweater. As I rounded the corner in the passageway, I literally ran into three girls. Oh, my God! There was the girl I had seen on the pier! She was every bit as cute as I remembered. Brownish blond hair, blue eyes, and a petite, but great, body. With all the charm I could muster, I introduced myself and invited all three girls to join me for the movie. Lucky for me, the other two said they still were under the weather, but if Marian wanted to go, that was fine with them.

We went to the movie and then to the nightclub with Thomas and Harris. We did a lot of dancing cheek to cheek and it was mutually apparent that some real chemistry was at work. Marian was a Southern girl (which perhaps explained her good looks, charm and pose, something that so many Yankee girls seemed to lack) from North Carolina. Her family was in the textile business and was apparently quite wealthy. What was important was that she had the same feelings for me as I did for her. I could see it in her eyes and in her body language: that intangible enthusiasm that says you are special to me.

After the nightclub closed, I walked Marian back to her cabin and as we kissed good night, she promised to be my girl for the rest of the voyage. I cannot tell you how overjoyed I was at that time, but little did I know what was to follow.

I spent the next day almost exclusively with Marian, laughing and talking. We had lunch, sunbathed in the afternoon, and after dinner went to the nightclub. My cabin mates and I had previously planned a "Vino" party since the wine onboard was only $1.25 a bottle. As if that weren't enough cause for celebration, it was bubbly and tasted a lot like champagne.

Marian and I left the club early and headed for the cabin. We found a cozy spot on my bunk bed, had some wine and joined in the merriment. Maybe it was the wine, or perhaps the beer at the club, but Marian began to confess that there were some serious problems causing her to have very guilty feelings.

It seems that back in North Carolina there was not just a boyfriend, but a fiancé. She had never in her wildest dreams thought that she would meet someone else. Her two girlfriends, both from her home town, had seen how much time she was spending with me and were also laying on the guilt trip, as they knew and liked her fiancé. They had discouraged her from socializing, which explained why it took me so long to find her, and were now very upset.

Marian told me that she was not fast or promiscuous (I knew that was true without her telling me) and what she felt for me was very real. In fact, she was frightened of her feelings and terribly ashamed for "cheating" on her boy back home, even though we

37

had only kissed and snuggled. Finally, she said it really wouldn't be right to keep seeing each other because there was too much attraction between us, and if we continued, something more would happen that we both might live to regret. Deep down, I knew she was right, because I certainly wanted her to be mine— both physically and emotionally. I told her I respected her honesty and her feelings and I walked her back to her cabin. With a hug, we said goodbye.

Marian's revelation stunned me. After years of hit and miss, I had finally been on the verge of a truly great relationship with someone I might eventually marry. Marian had all the great qualities I was hoping for in a wife: good looks, class, intelligence, sincerity and that magical chemistry that bonds two people together through good times and bad. However, it was all for naught. There was much more to this story to come, but on that evening, I resigned myself to a future without Marian.

The next day, I made a point not to see Marian. I sunbathed alone that afternoon, not even with Thomas or Harris. Sharon stopped by to offer to do some washing for me, which I greatly appreciated.

After dinner, I went to the club with the guys and had a few beers while we played cards. I didn't say much about Marian, but it was obvious that something was amiss so they tried to cheer me up. As we were playing,

I noticed that Thomas, who was directly across the table, suddenly looked up with a somewhat startled expression.

I turned to see Marian standing alone across the room staring at me and smiling softly. She walked toward me, so I stood to watch her approach. She spoke first, asking if I could talk for a few minutes. I was shocked to see her, but in another way, I wasn't that surprised. Gathering my wits, I managed to express my agreement. After excusing myself from the card game, we walked out of the club together. She reached for and held my hand as we walked to the front of the ship's deck where we could see the ship's bow slicing the waves in the moonlight.

Marian started the conversation with a simple question: Was I upset at her for what she had said the night before? I told her that I fully understood her dilemma and appreciated her honesty. She seemed greatly relieved and we spent a long time talking about our relationship, how much it meant to her (and to me) and what a "mess" it had created with her emotions. It was obvious that she was falling in love with me, but, at the same time, fighting with all her strength to keep me out of her thoughts. She knew that when the voyage and summer were over, she would be going back to North Carolina and to her boyfriend and that I would be going back to Oklahoma and to Med school. She laughed when I told her that if I had wings, I would swoop her up, carry her home in my arms, and never allow her to go back to North Carolina. We both knew that this could never happen.

Our serious conversation left no time for romance. For no apparent reason she began to cry and as I wiped away her tears, she apologized for making such a fool of herself. I told that hadn't happened. She abruptly said she had to go. Without saying goodbye, she ran back to her cabin alone.

When I awoke the next morning, I realized it was Sunday, so I decided not to get up until I damn well wanted. As I about to slip back into sleep, I became barely conscious of someone gently rapping on our cabin door. Everyone else was asleep, so I rolled out of bed and cracked open the door.

Marian was standing there looking lovely in a Sunday-go-to-church dress and heels. She asked if I would take her to the ship's Sunday church service and, of course, I said I would love to but needed some time to get ready. Although it was a sudden change in plans, it was well worth it.

It was a beautiful day at sea and after the services, we took our lunch out on the deck. It was so pleasant to see Marian in a happy mood and share conversation that wasn't so serious. She was her sweet, smiling, lovely self once again, with no ifs and buts. We spent

40

the afternoon talking in the sun and reading. Even though we were simply spending time together, it was very pleasant and filled me with happiness and a feeling that things might work out.

Although we didn't make definite plans for later, I assumed that I would see her after dinner (we had assigned seating at different tables) at the club. Several student-passengers had organized a variety show that would be something fun for us to see.

Marian never came to the club nor to the show. I left early and went to her cabin concerned that she might have taken ill. Her two girl friends met me at the doorway with sour looks on their faces. They declared that Marian was not feeling well and that it would be best for me to go away and leave her alone. I told them that I had never made her do anything that she didn't want to do, and pleaded with them to let me talk to her. They told me that Marian didn't want to talk to me. Although I knew they were lying, I thought it would be unwise to force the issue, so I left.

The next day we spotted the distant shoreline of France. We were scheduled to arrive in Amsterdam the next morning. Although I kept looking for Marian, she was nowhere to be found. Finally, I joined my four cabin mates lying in the sun. We were all in our boxer style swimsuits as were all the other guys. Quite unexpectedly, someone leaned over my shoulder to whisper, "Hello."

It was Marian (who else?) and I made room for her at my side. She had on a very cute two-piece suit with ruffles across the bra to make her boobs look bigger, which she really didn't need since she amply filled a C cup. We talked for a while with no mention of the previous night. Then, in a very private whisper, she asked if we could go to my cabin since she had something very private to tell me.

We excused ourselves and scurried down the appropriate corridors into the always-unlocked room. Sprawled on my lower bunk, Marian smiled sweetly and cuddled up to me. She began talking in a soft voice and asked that no matter what happened next, would I promise not to take advantage of her. She said she was a virgin and would I please respect her wishes to remain so.

This really caught me by surprise since we had never come close to having sex. I replied that, of course, I would respect her wishes and would protect her. She seemed completely at ease with my assurance and we began to kiss passionately and express our passion with every inch of our bodies. I cannot tell you how great it felt to have her warm, soft lips, tongue, and body melting into mine. I ran my hand down her back, across the hollow above her hip and pulled her bottom toward me. We lay for a while tightly clenched and then rolled slightly over so that she was on her back. I ran my hand across her tummy and while we kissed, I slid my hand down further and further until it eased beneath her swim suit into the soft silky hair. A little gasp escaped her sweet lips, but she offered no resistance.

I really didn't know much about female anatomy, but I did know that there was a very sensitive area at the upper part of the lips, so I began to gently rub this area using her natural moisture for lubrication. Almost instantly, I could feel her entire body tense and soon she began moaning softly with her face pressed into the curve of my neck. As her body tension escalated, I likewise increased my rubbing but was very careful to be gentle. For several seconds it seemed as if she became totally rigid and unable to breathe. This was a little scary to me, so I slid my hand out and asked her if she was alright. Her reply was a soft nod, then asked me to please hold her tightly. I gripped her pelvis snugly, pulling her close as she slipped into a wonderful rubbing rhythm with her thighs and body. I soon exploded into a breathtaking orgasm, filling the inside of my swimsuit with warm, slippery juice.

For several minutes we laid wrapped up in each other's arms, saying nothing, just bathing in the sweet afterglow. Suddenly the unlocked door smashed open as Ray rushed into the cabin. I rolled over, shaking my fist as I told him to get the hell out. He gasped, apologized, and left the cabin at breakneck speed.

I turned to find Marian sitting up and adjusting her swimsuit. Obviously, the magic of the moment had been shattered. She spoke in a soft but deliberate voice, almost as if she had rehearsed the words many times.

She told me that I was the most wonderful guy she had ever met. That something about me was very special and that if only she had met me several months earlier things could be so much different. But (how I hated the sound of that word) she had made a sacred commitment to the boy back home and she was honor bound not to break it. Therefore, it would be impossible for us to continue, as it would only bring pain to both of us. With the distinctive tone of finality in her voice, she declared that we must not see each other again. She would stay with her friends at the ship's farewell party that night and I should stay with mine. She had arranged to return on an earlier sailing so that there would be no chance of us being together again.

And so, for the third time, I was rejected. I suppose I had subconsciously prepared myself because of what had transpired earlier. I knew that there was no way she could go home and tell her family that she met a guy aboard the ship and that she was dropping out

44

of school, breaking her engagement, and running off to Oklahoma, which was still the Wild West to many people. Maybe such things happen in the movies or books, but not in real life. Marian did leave me with one great moment of happiness to remember her by, and I believe it was just as great a moment for her as well.

That evening I did not attempt to see or talk to Marian. When I glimpsed her from a distance looking my way, I quickly shifted my gaze.

The next morning as we left the ship, I never saw her in the crowd of disembarking people. I had resigned myself that I would never see her again. I was *almost* right.

PART FOUR: THE ADVENTURE

We will have these moments to remember...

Moments to Remember
by the *Four Lads* was a popular song
of the '50s that eloquently voiced the
emptiness of friendships separated by
the passage of time.

Europe!

After clearing customs, we boarded a student bus that took us to our hotel in Amsterdam. The city was different than I had imagined—it was quite clean, and the people were friendly and many spoke English. Beautiful canals and bridges graced the landscape. As if that weren't enough, a bicycle race scheduled for the next morning added an air of excitement.

Even in the '50s, Amsterdam's red light district was well known. The three of us decided to scout the area on the first evening in order to prepare for the real business the next night. It was difficult to admit that we were all neophytes, so the preliminary rehearsal was a way to fake it, so to speak.

My limited experience in the USA hadn't prepared me for what we discovered. There were no bellhops to tip to get a girl; instead, Mecca came to us. Window after window exposed attractive girls calling like the Sirens to Ulysses. Since we knew our erotic desires were well within reach, we returned to the hotel filled with anticipation.

The next day we attended a guided tour through the canals of Amsterdam and visited the great Rijhs museum. After supper and a German classical music open-air concert, it was time for our big move to the red light district. Since it was quite safe to walk alone at night, the plan was to peer into the windows until one of us found someone appealing, then split up and meet back at the hotel.

I was the first to spot a desirable girl. When I saw her pretty blue eyes through the window, I knew she was the one. She had a gentle, unhardened look, much like many of the girls we had seen in the shops and stores. I quickly bid adieu to Thomas and Harris and knocked on the door while they meandered down the street.

The blue-eyed girl opened the door, recognized me as an American, and invited me inside in English. She told me that her charge would be about $4 and asked if that was agreeable. I quickly said yes, so she asked me to follow her up to her room. As we started up the stairs, I could see into the kitchen where apparently her family was having coffee. Although I found it interesting, I was far too excited to dwell on our cultural differences!

As we entered her room and shut the door, she

went to her bedside table, opened the drawer, and offered a European brand rubber. I thanked her, but said I had one of my own. She smiled and began to undress, removing her dress and panties, but leaving on her bra and bobby sox. I thought this was rather strange, but assumed it must be a European custom.

I put her money on the night stand and quickly stripped. As she lay on her bed with her legs invitingly spread apart, it wasn't long until I could easily roll on the rubber. I climbed between her legs, but before I did anything else, she dipped her fingers into her mouth, and then moistened the end of my rubber-covered erection with saliva. She said this would help my entrance and as predicted, I easily slid into her warm opening. We were soon humping together with a nice rhythm. As my orgasm drew near, she began to moan softly as if she too was about to climax. Even though I knew she was faking, it added to my excitement and orgasmic enjoyment.

Afterward she took my spent rubber and flushed it down the toilet. As I washed in her sink she quickly dressed and seemed to enjoy watching me dress. As we started down the stairs, she asked if I'd like to meet her family. Shocked at such a request, I could only mumble a quiet agreement. Soon a brightly smiling family—her mother, father, brother, and sister— greeted me! Finally, after we conversed several minutes in English, the blue-eyed girl told them I needed to go and they politely excused me. As she walked me to the door she asked if I would come back to see her and, of course, I said I would. Half-stunned by the unexpected reception, I wandered back to the hotel to share my story with Thomas and Harris.

Although we were in Amsterdam two more days, I never got the chance to see the blue-eyed girl again. Our bicycle trip to a nearby village to see windmills and wooden shoes consumed one day and fulfilled our obligation to the Holland-American's shore excursion tours. Free to roam, the next day we took a train to Paris.

We arrived in Paris at Garde de Nord station in the early evening and found a hotel nearby. For only $2 each, we had a bath adjoining our room and a shower down the hall. We enjoyed dinner at a small French café and decided to go for a walk. We hoped to find Pig-Alle, since our hormones had been dormant for a few days and were surging once again.

Pig-Alle was not as bawdy as I had imagined—it was mostly clip joints and a few bars. At first, we didn't see anyone decent looking, but eventually we spotted a cute little blonde who appeared to be in business. I told Thomas and Harris that I had "dibs" and they said "fine." They agreed to meet me back at the hotel and continued to look.

The blonde was about my age, maybe a couple of years older. She was neat and clean, with an attractive face and a nice body. I asked her if she spoke English and she said yes. I told her I was looking for a 'date' and asked if she were interested. She smiled and replied yes once again. After a brief conversation I discovered the price was approximately $8 in American money. She said she lived nearby and that we could go to her place. I replied that it seemed fine with me, so we headed down a side street, entered a small apartment building, took two flights of stairs, and arrived at a small one-room apartment.

There was a bed, some chairs, a small table and a kitchenette. Through an open door, I could see a tiny room with a sink, toilet, and bidet. She pulled down the bed covers, asked me to put the money on the table, and told me to undress and put my clothes on one of the chairs.

While I happily obeyed, she counted the money, put it in her purse, and undressed except for her bra, which she left on like the girl in Amsterdam. Again, I thought this must be some European custom—to get in bed and have sex without being completely naked. Maybe on a busy evening this helped speed up the turnover time.

She had a nice body and as I saw her lying with her legs spread wide, my manhood reacted like Pavlov's

53

dog did when the bell chimed. I had remembered to bring a rubber, which I rolled into place and quickly climbed into the proverbial saddle. After no more than a minute, she whispered in my ear something to the effect that I was so big and she was so little, perhaps it would be best if she got on top. My first thought was that the French must have little weenies, but then it dawned on me she was referring to my body size (185 pounds and 6 feet tall). Although disappointed at my logical conclusion I, nevertheless, agreed to make the switch and she was quickly on top with me firmly inside.

To this day, I cannot really explain the pulsating, vibrating motion that emanated from that small, petite body. It certainly sent me into ecstasy far too soon, with the wish it could have lasted much longer. As soon as she sensed I had released my intensity, she rolled off and directed me to the sink where she said I could clean up. I flushed the rubber down the toilet, washed with bar soap and water, dried with a small towel and quickly dressed.

She walked me back to Pig-Alle, thanked me for the money, and said if I was ever back in Paris to look her up. Oh, my God! What a delightful thought!

No one was at the hotel when I got back and I wasn't surprised since I had taken first choice. When they did return, I told them every detail of my extraordinary experience. I also had the feeling that they doubted my story, since their stories were much more mundane. I didn't argue the point, but later that night before I fell asleep, I felt a great degree of smugness and self-satisfaction because I knew I had told them the truth.

The next day we moved to an even cheaper hotel near the American Embassy. We quickly discovered we could eat lunch at the embassy for only 60 cents—a real deal! Thomas and I also found out we could get a later sailing (5 days!) and transferred to that date. Since Harris had to get back, he kept his original schedule. The extra days would allow us to spend a couple of days in London before returning, which Thomas and I thought would be worthwhile—little did we know exactly how worthwhile it would be!

After leaving the embassy, we went to the car rental garage where Thomas had made reservations for our European adventure. The owner was very nice and for $120 each we rented the car for the next 6 weeks. If we went over 10,000 kilometers we would have to pay more, but we assured him that would not be the case. The car was really neat: a little four door Citroen with a small but adequate trunk. It looked like a miniature version of a black gangster sedan. It was not the common model, which looked like a rolling washboard with its ugly corrugated front. We told the owner we wanted to spend a little more time in Paris and we would be back in two days to pay him and pick up the car. With the deal set, we left excited.

With the ship and car arrangements made, we were free to spend two days seeing the marvelous sights of Paris. We began with a bus orientation of the city and embraced the usual tourist stuff. The bus driver announced a nightclubbing event that evening and invited us to join the group if we wished. It sounded like a good deal and turned out to be a great one.

After supper, we met his group and off we went, first to the Follies Berger's (a very beautiful show) and then to the Moulin Rouge where we enjoyed champagne as the can-can girls put on a great floorshow. We wound up the evening at a small jazz club with more champagne. We even had a long, friendly conversation with "Sugar" Ray Robinson, the famous boxer, who was at the table next to ours. Finally, we arrived back at the hotel at 3:00 A.M. It had been a wonderful night, especially for only $11.50 each!

When we went out the next day, there were flags everywhere. The one on the Arc de Triomphe must have been 60 feet high. In our naivety, we had not realized it was Bastille Day, the French equivalent of the Fourth of July! Since we were leaving Paris the next morning, we made the most of the holiday. Throngs of celebrating people added to the excitement as we squeezed in every possible attraction the city still had to offer.

As we headed south in our great little Citroen toward the Chateau region, I reflected on the trip to date. Although Paris was very old, its ornate architecture and young, vital population made it a truly beautiful city. Lovers were everywhere—hugging, kissing, holding hands, and looking deeply in each other's eyes completely oblivious to the rest of the world. The French women were quite attractive and it was obvious that, unlike their American counterparts, many wore little or no undies. The men were quite short; in fact, every French person was short. Most were friendly and pleasant, but anyone who raised a finger to help in a café, hotel, museum, or anywhere always expected a reward for their service. Such tipping was most unlike the Netherlands and Amsterdam.

Two other things struck me as somewhat bizarre: the large number of "Bohemians" with their long scruffy beards (the forerunner of "hippies") and the open public toilets. The men's version was open at the bottom and top with only the middle area covered. One could converse with whomever on the outside while relieving oneself on the inside: very strange indeed for the American sensibility.

We spent the next 3½ days visiting chateaus, old cities, and Roman ruins in Central and Southern France. The countryside was most picturesque with wheat farms, vegetable gardens, and flowered arbors. The villages had many small houses with plastered walls and orange tiled roofs. Everything I had heard about the French countryside was true, including the amazing tree-lined highways. The roads were all two-lane (no four-lane parkways) and for miles and miles neatly spaced trees graced both sides of the road. I wondered if a French "Johnny Appleseed" had obsessively planted trees along the roads!

When we reached the French Riviera near Cannes we headed straight for the beach. It was a warm, sunny afternoon, and we spent the rest of the day in the sand and water. All the women wore skimpy two-piece swimsuits called "bikinis" which left little to the imagination. The men wore short trunks cut like briefs that reminded me of the Yale swimming team. Of course, we were in our American boxer-like trunks and were probably the blunt of many French jokes about modest Americans.

After supper, we returned to the deserted beach, spread towels on the sand, and watched the stars appear. We talked for hours. Since it was warm and pleasant lying in the fresh ocean air, we decided "to hell with a hotel." Instead, we camped on the beach that night. A public shower was nearby, so the next morning we washed off the sand and headed down the coast.

We spent the next two days going from one city to another along the French, Monaco, and Italian Rivieras. There was always time for a swim and sunning. The Italian Riviera was not as nice as the French—the roads were rough and the cities were more congested. There was definitely a different feeling in Italy that was hard to describe. Perhaps it was a touch of melancholy in the people. At the end of the second day, we reached Pisa, where we spent the night.

Since our hotel was only a block from the Leaning Tower, we went early the next morning for the sole purpose of climbing the tower. It was a beautiful, sunny day and after paying the entrance fee we scrambled up the inner stairway to the top. It is a shame that the government no longer allows tourists this privilege, since the view was terrific. Next to the tower was a large basilion or cathedral. Unlike the French cathedrals, it was Romanesque with an enormous glinting bronze dome. We visited a nearby Baptistery that had fabulous acoustic qualities. By the time we left, we felt that the surrounding buildings were more fabulous than the famous Leaning Tower!

By noon, we were on our way to Florence. After finding a hotel, we met an English-speaking gentleman who offered to act as a free guide through the city. What a deal! The tour the next day was spectacular— we visited fabulous statues, cathedrals, and museums. I highly recommend that everyone seize the opportunity to experience the wonderful city of Florence!

Next our guide escorted us to a leather working shop. We bought some boxes and billfolds for gifts for family and friends. To show our appreciation, we each gave our guide a pack of cigarettes and fifty lira (about 9 cents) to pay for his supper. He was delighted and repeatedly thanked us.

As we had done in Holland and France, we decided to spend the evening in search of eager Italian women. Since we were unaware of any red light districts, we began driving around to see if we could find a lonesome streetwalker eager for action. Within a block of our hotel, I spotted a slender, young gal overtly advertising her availability. Since I saw her first, I called "dibs" first, and Thomas and Harris agreed to drop me off and look elsewhere.

As I approached, she smiled and I asked her if she spoke English. She said she did, so I asked her what she would charge for a "date" (same old line). The price was fine (about $4) and I suggested that we go to my hotel, which was only about a block away. She said that would be okay, so we strolled off holding hands like best of friends.

Once we entered the room, she asked for the money and put it into her purse. As she began to undress (even the bra!) it became apparent that what had seemed to be a lovely, petite girl, was not so. Her breasts were flat, small, and sagging as if all the inner substance was gone. Her skinny, bony body had stretch marks across the belly, apparently from giving birth. Even though she wasn't much to look at, something was better than nothing, so I undressed, donned my rubber and climbed atop her spread out body.

She was too dry to penetrate, so I "greased up" with a little saliva and slid inside. She made no effort whatsoever to participate in what I was hoping would be an experienced and dynamic performance. It was as if I was using her vagina to relieve my sexual tension and nothing more. Sort of like masturbation using her body parts. The act bore no resemblance to the girls in Paris or Amsterdam.

Afterward as I was washing up, I saw her over my shoulder rummaging in Harris's suitcase. As I turned around, I saw her take some candy bars and I yelled for her to put them back, that they weren't mine. She was obviously startled, but put them back and boldly asked if I had anything I would give her. This caught me by surprise, so I suggested a couple of packs of American cigarettes. She agreed, so I grabbed the packs and quickly escorted her out of the hotel. I told her goodbye and didn't look back. I didn't care where she went, hoped she wasn't typical of Italian women, and returned to the lobby to wait for my friends.

Only fifteen or twenty minutes passed before they came back. They said they hadn't had much luck and gave up. I told them about my lousy lay and that she was both a dud and a thief. This led to a long conversation about women and sex and whether it was worth the time and effort to get laid in every country we visited. We finally agreed that we would no longer rely on women of the night. Unless the opportunity presented itself for a roll with a nice girl, there would be no roll at all. No more paying for sex…After all, we were good-looking, athletic guys who shouldn't have to pay!

As the conversation progressed, Thomas and Harris reluctantly confessed that they had chickened out in Amsterdam and Paris. I was the only one who had had the guts to approach and procure a woman. Although they were horny, red-blooded guys, they just couldn't muster the desire (or courage) to pay for sex.

This came as a shock to me, but I remembered how difficult it was for me the first time I had such an experience. The summer after my freshman year I had gone with two friends in Oklahoma City to a hotel known for call girls. One friend had been there before and showed the two of us what to do. First, he went to the hotel porter and asked if he could get a girl for the three of us. The porter said he could, but we would have to rent a room. We all chipped in and our "leader" got the room. We tipped the porter and anxiously waited in the room.

Soon a woman ten years our senior knocked on the door and came in. The porter said it would cost us $10 each, but the woman wanted $15, so we said okay. We then flipped coins to see who went first—I was second. While each took a turn, the other two waited in the hall. It was sort of scary and hard to get a good erection. Since we all used rubbers, it wasn't messy, but it wasn't the greatest, either. Nevertheless, the three of us held a reunion the next two summers and the third time it was no problem at all. To this day, it remains something I've never really felt great about or wanted to share with anyone.

Consequently, when Thomas and Harris confessed, I completely understood. If I had known, I would have helped them like my friend helped me, but I had falsely assumed they were experienced. As we continued to talk, it became clear that they regarded me as sort of a Casanova. Apparently, Bob had spread the word that I was screwing Marian onboard the ship after he walked in on us. Even though that wasn't true, I began to understand where they were coming from. In any event, they thought I had a real active "dick" and began to tease me a little about me being so horny. When they threatened to call me "Dick," I replied, "If you do I'll call you Tom and Harry." Amid lots of chuckles we became Tom, Dick, and Harry for the rest of the summer.

We had not planned to spend further time in Florence before moving on, but some bastard threw a rock through our rear window, so we stayed an extra day for repairs. Even three days were not enough to witness everything Florence had to offer, so the extra day was well worthwhile. Unfortunately, someone stole "Tom's" camera and our auto battery died. Replacing it brought back not-so-fond memories of the Hard Times Buick! The extra day was nice, but expensive. We left in the early evening and spent the night in Sienna before proceeding to Rome.

Rome was a blur of fascinating people and places as we crammed what most people would do in a week or more into three days. Being young, energetic, and in excellent shape allowed us to zip around without much rest. Everything in Rome was fabulous, but a few things deeply etched my memory.

At the Arch of Titus, we learned that no Jew had ever passed through the arch. Since we weren't Jewish, we had no problem walking under it. We learned that the reason no Jew had ever passed through was that the split second they did; they were no longer Jewish.

Apparently, Titus and Hitler were two of a kind.

We saw several of Michelangelo's fantastic marble statues, but the most impressive of all was in St. Peter in Chains, a little church where his sculpture of Moses resided. Its anatomical detail was extraordinary—veins, tendons, and muscles were so expertly carved they seemed to be real. In the good old USA, we would construct a huge building to protect such a treasure, but in Rome it was housed in a niche in a small church. Impressive treasures filled the city of Rome.

On the second afternoon as we were scurrying down the street, I saw a tourist bus loading a group of American girls. Oh, my God! I said to myself. That's Marian!

I began walking fast, almost running, toward her while one by one the girls disappeared into the bus. Just as she was about to board, she saw me waving and calling her name. At first, she smiled, but then she became a little flustered. Just as I breathlessly arrived, she boarded the bus.

I stood beside the bus as she took a window seat and glanced to see if I was still there. As the bus pulled away, she flashed a melancholy smile and looked away. She disappeared from my life forever that day. I never saw or heard from her again. I have often thought of her, wondering what path life led her down. In my mind,

I believe she returned to her hometown boyfriend, married him, and had his children. Although I cannot answer why, something tells me they eventually divorced. In my heart, I hope she found happiness.

We left Rome after 4 days and headed for the Adriatic coast. Three and a half days of visiting churches, artwork, statues, monuments, and ruins had left us reeling. It felt wonderful to be winding along mountain roads beside a jade green river. We arrived at the Adriatic at Fano and spent much of the afternoon at a beautiful sandy beach that was even better than the one at the French Riviera.

As we traveled north up the coastline, we saw a rather unusual sight in the early evening hours. About five or six miles inland was a small mesa-like mountain sitting alone in the flatland. The lights of a small city glittered on top. Our Italian map revealed that we were within sight of San Marino, a small communist country. Intrigued, we turned inland. We drove for about ten minutes, ascending the winding road that led to a quaint and picturesque little city. To our surprise, there were no border guards or passport checks, just friendly people. We drove around for a while, had a small evening meal, and found a bar.

Several Americans were in the bar, including a girl from Oklahoma whom I did not know. Thomas and Harris got rip roaring drunk and we all had a blast. Since I managed to stay sober, when we finally left, I drove. When I reached Remini on the coast, I dumped my friends on the beach where we spent the night covered only by the moonlight and our traveling clothes.

The following morning we enjoyed a swim, even though Harris was still drunk from the night before and Thomas had a hangover. In fact, Harris didn't really sober up until that afternoon! We reached Venice about 4:00 p.m. After parking and locking the car in a big lot, we took a gondola ride into Venice, which is basically an island quite near the shore, for three packs of cigarettes. We found a hotel for $5.40 ($1.80 each) and a barbershop where I paid two packs for a haircut.

We raced around the next day, experiencing the sights of Venice as well as riding a "bus boat" down the Grande Canal. While the main canals were clean and neat, many of the small canals were nasty and dirty. Venice was a lovely city, but it was dotted with tourist shops unlike anything we'd seen in Rome or Florence.

We left Venice in the late afternoon and reached Verona that evening. A performance of an open-air opera was underway in an old Roman arena, and even though none of us cared much for opera, it just seemed like the thing to do. I must reluctantly admit that it was a beautiful production and I enjoyed without understanding a word they sang or said. Afterward it was too late to look for a hotel, so we spent the night in a vineyard!

We must have been exhausted, since we didn't wake up until 9 a.m. the next morning. Apparently, the dirt in a vineyard is conducive to sleep because we enjoyed a wonderful rest and awoke completely refreshed. We arrived in Milan just after noon and marveled at the Gothic Cathedral that seemed even more elaborate than the one at Notre Dame. We tried to see The Last Supper inside St. Marie della Grazie, but son of a bitch, it was closed!

After we left Milan and headed north, the beautiful Swiss Alps were visible in the far distance. We then vowed to take a vacation from the cultural aspects of our journey. We arrived at Lake Como in northern Italy that evening, found a cheap hotel overlooking the beautiful water, and spent the evening flicking out, which was our college expression for watching movies. The American movie was in Italian, but we enjoyed it anyway. We met some American girls who were staying in a swanky hotel called Villa D'este and we agreed to meet them the next day.

Mere words cannot express how pleasant it was to sail around Lake Como in a rented sailboat. We packed bread, cheese, salami, and wine and had lunch aboard our skiff while absorbing the sunshine and the view of the distant, snow-covered Swiss Alps.

True to our word, we met the American girls at their hotel after dinner. While none were true beauties, they were friendly and sweet. It was great to have conversations in English again! We didn't know where to go or what to do, so we wound up playing bridge in the hotel game room.

One of the girls was from Texas University. As we became acquainted, I mentioned that I had lived in Paris, Texas for about a year while I was in the 5th grade. She said she was familiar with some girls from Paris and, lo and behold, she knew my very first girl friend, Sue Ann Hedges! I say my very first girlfriend because Sue Ann really lit up my light. The Army briefly stationed my Dad there during WWII. At ten years old, I was just beginning to feel an attraction toward girls.

When I saw Sue Ann, I knew she was the one! I heard that John Oxford, the richest boy in Paris, was supposedly her boyfriend, but I didn't care. I seized every opportunity to talk to her—I'd tell her about my dog, and ask everything I could about her life and family. At least a month went by before I realized she only lived three houses away.

Truly smitten, I would watch for her and walk

to school at her side. The weekends found me at her house on the slightest pretense. We soon became dear friends, John was out of the picture, and although we were too young to date, we had a "date" to go to Sunday school every weekend.

I was madly in love with her when my father received orders transferring him to Carlisle, PA. I was heartsick. I'm not sure if we ever kissed, but I will never forget the goodbye hug we shared when I had to leave. I am still amazed that I found someone in Europe who knew Sue Ann—it really is a small world! I asked if she still had beautiful blonde hair and blue eyes. She replied that she was as pretty as ever and that she was pinned to a guy from Texas University. I knew he was a lucky guy, since Sue Ann was a really wonderful person. After bridge, we talked to the girls until the wee hours of the night but there was no romance.

As we headed toward Switzerland the next day, we found another lake with a great beach where we could swim and sun, Lake Maggiore. It wasn't as nice as Lake Como, so we hit the road again, arriving at the Swiss border late that afternoon.

Switzerland was more beautiful than any photo could ever convey. After driving into the mountains, which were right at the frontier, we found an Inn that offered a free place to sleep if we had our own sleeping bags. We had brought them along since the nights were often chilly, and we discovered some old mattresses in our stable-like room. We spent our first night in the Alps in Boy Scout comfort, but the price was definitely right!

The next day we decided to go to Lake Geneva. The drive was spectacular—through a beautiful mountain pass that descended into a river valley and the lake. The air was crisp and clean, a perfect day to travel. By the time we arrived at Montreux on the edge of Lake Geneva, the mountains were in the distance. The town was crowded with European tourists but we did finally find an inexpensive hotel. We spent the afternoon at the lake, swimming, sunning and relaxing. Although it was a great place, it wasn't quite as nice as Lake Como. We found a casino that evening and did some big time gambling. I lost one Swiss franc (23 cents) while Thomas and Harris each lost 8 francs. It was great fun, especially watching the people.

I awoke the next morning sick as a dog; vomiting, diarrhea, aching all over. Thomas and Harris brought all kinds of pills and paregoric but nothing seemed to work. Later that day Thomas started to get sick as well, but fortunately wasn't as severely stricken. After a horrible, miserable day, I was felt a bit better that evening and managed to keep down a little soup and a poached egg. I slept like a baby that night, thankful the worst seemed to be over.

Since we all felt fine in the morning, we were off again! The hotel clerk had told us about a remote area called Val de Foully near the French-Italian border that was, in his opinion, a wonderful place to spend a few days away from the crowds and hubbub. Another mountain ascent led us to our destination on narrow backwoods roads. Indeed, it was quite beautiful there—steep mountains, lush meadows, and cascading mountain streams. We found an Inn that resembled a hunting lodge for only $3.50 each, including meals.

Since it was still daylight, we raced to the slopes like wild mountain goats, leaping across 6 to 8 foot wide streaming waterfalls where a miscalculation or stumble would have been catastrophic. Of course, we were young, strong, and without a care in the world, so we didn't waste a moment worrying about things that might not happen! Foolish, probably...but I would do it again in a heartbeat. For that moment, we were three wild animals frolicking in wilderness unlike anything we had ever experienced.

Early the next morning we packed a lunch of canned meat, bread, and chocolate candy, then headed down a trail that led to a tarn, or a mountain lake. We arrived shortly after noon, enjoyed lunch, and explored a little. The view from the lake was spectacular—snow covered Alps in the background, glaciers in front, and a valley below with a stream fed by snow and ice melted water. While hiking back, we crossed several areas in the clouds and drank pure, clean water from mountain streams.

We left the Inn the next morning, angry as hell because the woman innkeeper had added "extras" to our bill that we didn't use. Our hard feelings melted away, however, as we drove to St. Bernard, where we visited the dogs in their kennels and toured the museum. We also bought a little brandy to sustain us, since it was a lousy, rainy day.

Our destination was Interlaken in the German speaking area of Switzerland. As we neared the region, the style of homes changed to the picture book Swiss houses with lush flower boxes in the windows. The villages and farms were unbelievably picturesque and Interlaken was also very nice, but overrun with tourists.

The next day we drove to Zurich, did a little window-shopping, then headed for the German border. As we drove out of the Alps, past customs and into the farm country of Southern Germany, we began to see a little war damage. We had a road detour because of construction, but Harris (who was driving) thought we could make it across okay. Unfortunately, we came to a crashing halt when the right front tire dropped into an 18" hole. We were able to shove the car out of the hole, but the tire was blown and the wheel bent. Luckily, we had a spare tire and wheel in the trunk to use as a replacement. We stashed the broken wheel under the mat, where it may still be today. Yes, we should have told the Frenchman from whom we rented the car about the wheel, but he didn't ask!

We made it to Freiberg that evening which was on the edge of the Black Forest. We had a great bratwurst supper and drank fine German beer. Most Germans spoke a little English and my four semesters of German at Yale made communicating much easier than it had been in France, Italy, and Switzerland.

Our next destination was Heidelberg, which took us through the Black Forest. Once again, it was a rainy day, but the gloominess provided the perfect setting for the Black Forest. Appropriately named, the tall, dark pines loomed on the gray, rocky hillsides. The number of hills surprised me, as did the fact that most of forest that seemed to be virgin timber. We could see glimpses of the Rhein Valley from time to time where the trees weren't so thick, but didn't clear the forest until Baden-Baden where we picked up the autobahn to Heidelberg.

We found a private home that took in guests and then headed for the famous Heidelberg beer halls. That evening's meal was another round of bratwurst and sauerkraut at the "Red Ox," where we passed around a clear glass boot of beer. Some of the American girls we met at Lake Como were there, so we struck up some old friendships but, again, romance wasn't in the air.

We heard there were towns east of Heidelberg that were over a thousand years old, so after touring the University and a few other historic sites, we spent the next two days visiting Dinklesbuhl, Rothenberg and Michelstadt. Entering the very old, but quaint, virtually medieval towns with ancient homes and buildings, cobblestone narrow streets, and wooden carts gave us the feeling that we had stepped back in time. Only the tourists had cars. The antiquated surroundings produced an eerie feeling that I wasn't sure I liked.

On the way back we picked up the Rhein River at Mainz, where we could still see ruins from the WWII allied bombing. Unlike France and Italy, the Germans were repairing and rebuilding like scalded ants. Even on Sunday, chemical plants were running full blast. It was a completely different attitude—no two hour afternoon "siestas" in Germany!

As we continued up the Rhein we saw castles and vineyards, but didn't stop for tours since we hoped to reach Luxembourg that evening. There we found a little hotel and had a supper that was quite different from our previous fare of wurst and beer. I'm sure we instantly began to smell better!

Luxembourg was interesting and unique. Once a

large fort, the old walls, towers, and casements were still in tact. There was also a fascinating labyrinth of tunnels carved out of solid rock. While some of them were still passable, but many had been destroyed over the years. At one time, the tunnels created a virtual honeycomb beneath the city. In addition to these marvels, some ancient Roman aqueducts were still in use.

On route to Reims we passed through Verdun, which gained fame as the greatest battle site of WWI. We saw many monuments to the clash between France and Germany that resulted in over 700,000 casualties, and an old French cemetery, but didn't have the time to give the city the attention it deserved. We reached Reims in the early evening and had time to visit its famous cathedral—perhaps the most beautiful one in all of France. Reims is in the center of champagne country and therefore it was as cheap as wine elsewhere in France. Of course, we spent a mellow evening sampling the fine local vintage.

On the road to Reims, it became apparent that the 10,000 kilometer limit on our rental Citroen was about to expire. Although not much of a mechanic, I managed to disengage the speedometer cable from the speedometer case. From then on, we drove without a functioning speedometer or mileage indicator. That wasn't a problem and it was certainly cheaper than paying overage charge. Once again, Americans triumphed over the French!

Unfortunately, it was time to head back to Paris. After packing enough champagne for lunch (along with bread, cheese and sausage), we left Reims in the morning. A brief stop in Epergne led to another champagne company tour, and they generously treated us to a bottle of their finest '47 vintage. This gesture made such an impression that I barely recall our visit to the palace at Fontainebleau, and am not certain what we saw besides the famous stair steps and Napoleon's suite.

By the time we arrived in Paris that evening, our minds were a bit clearer. We found a hotel in the student section for the bargain price of $1 per person per night. After sunset, we experienced the lights, people, homes, parks, and buildings of Paris from a different perspective by driving the city streets. I was tempted to search for the little blonde haired girl in Pig-Alle, but true to my word, I stayed with Thomas and Harris. To keep from sneaking away, I kept reminding myself that the second time one tastes of ambrosia is never as good as the first. The temptation was great, since even a little taste would have seemed very sweet at that point!

Hormones aside, we spent the next day taking advantage of the fact we still had wheels. Our visit to Versailles couldn't have happened on a more beautiful day. The splendor that was once France touched us all. Orange trees filled the spacious, carefully manicured gardens and we were allowed to peek into the "orangerie" a semi-cave (half below and half underground) where the orange trees were kept in the cold of winter.

On the way back we stopped at Sacre Coeur, a gorgeous church on a hill overlooking Paris. After parking the car, we walked to the Eiffel Tower, which was much taller than I had imagined. We were able to take the first elevator (on the slant) to the middle section as well as the second elevator to the top observation site. Of all the wild and crazy things we had experienced on our trip, the second elevator was the scariest. So much for French engineering! Nevertheless, the wonderful view of Paris was worth the worry. We stayed for at least half an hour before descending in the scare-cage.

Since we needed to return the rental car the next day, it was my job to crawl under the dashboard to reconnect the speedometer/odometer cable. Fortunately, it was an easy task and we returned the car in nice working order well under the 10,000 allowable kilometers. They reimbursed us for the battery, but since we hadn't purchased peril insurance, we had to pay for the windshield repair. We worried about the bent wheel and blown tire hidden beneath the floor panel in the trunk. Since our money was getting a little short, paying for it would have been a serious blow. We left the garage smiling that our secret went undiscovered, and never felt a twinge of guilt. Bad boys like us didn't care about such things.

We spent the rest of the day at the fabulous Louvre Museum captivated by the art and statues. The Mona Lisa was slightly disappointing—it was a small picture hanging in a long gallery of larger paintings. Nothing special designated the degree of her fame, and no crowd had formed to appreciate her. It was just another lonely piece of art in a hall full of less noteworthy counterparts.

Our spirits were as cold and damp as the weather as we headed back to the hotel to collect Harris's stuff. He was taking the evening train to Rotterdam, and then sailing home the next day. Thomas and I said our emotional good-byes to Harris at the station since were staying longer to visit London. Although we promised to write and keep in touch, I sensed that the brief window between our lives was closing forever. He had been a great friend, we had some fabulous times, and I will never forget him.

Thomas and I went back to the hotel, packed our bags, and had dinner at a very nice restaurant to help buoy our sagging spirits. We, too, were about to embark on the last leg of our adventure.

We slept late the next morning then checked out of the hotel. Since our train didn't leave until late that evening, we stowed our bags in a large locker at the station. A nearby movie theater was showing an American flick in English: *Take the High Ground*, which helped pass the time that afternoon. After a nice supper, we boarded the ten o'clock overnight train to London.

Even though we couldn't see much in the dark, we stayed awake, talking and watching the passing lights and shadows. We reached the English Channel at Dieppe around 1:00 a.m. where we transferred to a ferryboat that had bunk bed accommodations. We did get a little fitful sleep before reaching New Haven, England (an interesting coincidence for two Yalies so far from home!) at 4:30 a.m., where we boarded an English train that arrived at Victoria Station in London at 7:30 a.m.

Perhaps because we were back among English speaking people, we scarcely noticed that we had been up most of the night. We checked our bags in a locker and devoured an excellent American style breakfast of bacon and eggs for approximately 50 cents each. Our next stop was Victoria Street, where Thomas hoped to find an old Victorian house where he had lived one summer as a child. Although he knew the address, it wasn't very important to him since he remembered little about his time there. We eventually reached the Thames River and in succession we saw Big Ben, Westminster Abbey, Parliament, and #10 Downing Street. Since we weren't allowed to approach the home of the Prime Minister, we viewed the latter from the end of the block. Later we went across St. James Park to Buckingham Palace, watched the colorful "changing of the Guard," and finally wound up at Trafalgar Square with Admiral Nelson's statue and two beautiful fountains.

It was time to return to the train station to pick up our bags and find a hotel. On the way back we took a slight detour since Parliament had opened for guided tours. The building was an extremely large Gothic structure, while the actual rooms where the Lords and Commons met were relatively small. Although lavishly decorated, the building expressed a quiet dignity.

As we approached the station, we hunted for an inexpensive hotel. Since London was quite crowded, we were lucky to find a small hotel for only $1.65 each. It had once been a private home, and after settling into our cozy room, we had supper in the coffee shop and relaxed inside while it rained.

London was a special, wonderful city! The people on the streets were warm and friendly. They called us, "Yanks" which was okay, although my southern upbringing made me associated the word with "Yankee," a rather inflammatory word in our vocabulary. (Yes, the Civil War was still softly rumbling in 1954, just as it continues to do today.) The prices in England were quite reasonable. Although the food was a little bland, it was a welcome change from French "cuisine."

Finally, the rain stopped and we wandered back onto the street to ride a double-decker bus that looked top heavy but seemed stable enough. We stopped at a pub for beer and supper before returning to the hotel. It had been a very exciting day, in spite of our lack of sleep. As we went to bed, we were eagerly looking forward to two more days in London. Little did we know what awaited us!

Nice weather greeted us as we stirred the next morning. We decided to catch a bus to Windsor Castle, but quickly discovered that it was closed to the public on Sunday. Even so, we had a nice time wandering around the spacious lawns, gardens, and courtyards. Eton College was visible in the distance, and we walked to the nearby town to get a better view. Even though classes were out for the summer we still peeked into the buildings to see the old carved desks in the classrooms.

After returning to London, we headed for Westminster Bridge. We traveled on a sightseeing boat down the Thames to the old London Tower. Actually, the tower is not a tower at all—it's just a pentagonal fortress with multiple battlement towers. The main tower housed a museum containing old weapons, uniforms, and gear, but not a single crown jewel.

Since it was a beautiful day, we strolled along the bank of the Thames until we reached St. Paul's cathedral. It was huge and ornate, almost as big and beautiful as St. Peters in Rome. Because it was Sunday, we had complete access to the church. We had hoped to climb to the top of the dome, and were disappointed to learn that it was closed to the public.

After exploring the area, we caught a bus back to our hotel, had a nice supper for 81 cents, read a little in the lobby, and went to bed.

Since clothing was cheap in London, Thomas and I decided to do some shopping on our last day. Piccadilly Circus and Regent Street were rumored to have nice clothes, so we spent a chunk of the day exhaustively looking while only buying a few things— mostly sweaters (wool sweaters were only $4 to $6) for friends and family back home. Because English taste didn't coincide with American styles, we didn't find much for "shoe" Yalies!

After our shopping "spree," we visited Madame Trousseau's Wax Museum—an absolute must for the London visitor. The replica of President Eisenhower was fantastic, as were many of the other famous men and women of history.

Thomas and I had enjoyed a great buffet breakfast that morning and had forgotten about lunch. Since it was after 4:00 p.m., we began looking for a restaurant that offered a late lunch or early supper menu. Most of the Brits were drinking tea but we found a small cafeteria-like café serving food. We each grabbed a tray and as we moved through the line, we saw a cute dark haired girl. Since we were the only people in the food line, we immediately struck up a conversation. She graced us with her wonderful smile, and in the course of the brief conversation, we learned that her name was Sarah and that she wasn't married and didn't currently have a boyfriend.

Once we finished eating, we decided to ask her out. When Thomas and I returned to her station, she greeted us with that great smile. Since we decided I should do the talking, I asked if she would like to do something with us when she got off work. Not only did she say yes, it was an enthusiastic yes! She asked if her roommate, Jennifer, could join the fun, which was fine with us. We agreed we should all meet in front of the café at 8:30 that evening when she got off work.

After we left the café, Thomas and I were excited about the latest twist in our adventure. It had been a long time since either of us had been on a date with a nice girl. Sarah seemed both cute and sweet—a dream come true. However, Thomas stubbornly refused my request to have Sarah as my date, since he was afraid to be stuck with her roommate. We were both all too aware of the fact that good-looking girls often have not-so-good-looking roomies. I doubt if anyone knows why this phenomenon occurs—maybe it's a subconscious attempt to minimize competition. In any event, Thomas and I began a friendly argument over which one of us would date the yet-to-be-seen roommate, Jennifer.

As we walked and argued, I realized that my luck with women on our adventure had greatly surpassed his. After all, I had met Marian and had fantastic experiences with the girls in Amsterdam and Paris. A few twinges of guilt led me to agree that Thomas should be with Sarah that night while I escorted Jennifer, sight unseen. I rationalized my decision by convincing myself that she would probably decent looking and by reminding myself that Thomas had organized the entire European trip and graciously invited me to join in the fun. A blind date seemed to be the least I could do to repay him.

With over three hours to kill and nothing to do, we found a movie house showing newsreels (15 to 20 minute mini-movies about current events that were very popular in the '40s and '50s). Admission was one "Bob" (about 14 cents) which seemed more than reasonable, so we spent more than an hour catching up on the world events we had missed while traveling through Europe.

After the newsreels, we still time on our hands before meeting the girls, so we window- shopped and people-watched. Every minute dragged as our anticipation intensified. The closer it got to 8:30, the more time seemed to crawl.

Finally, it was time! As we rounded the corner, the two girls were waiting at the café's entrance. Sarah was in plain view, but the other girl had her back turned. I can't say beads of sweat were forming on my brow, but I was definitely apprehensive. As we drew closer, Sarah saw us, smiled, and waved. At that moment, Jennifer turned and I saw her for the first time.

Oh, my God! At the time, that was the only thing that registered. I had prepared myself for disappointment, so what I saw was a complete shock. Jennifer was gorgeous—blonde hair, blue eyes, beautiful skin, a wonderful smile, and a perfect figure. How lucky can one person get? It was as if the gods had rewarded me for my act of generosity toward Thomas!

I immediately introduced myself and told her that

I would be her date for the evening. She seemed to be very happy with the arrangement and Thomas and Sarah seemed pleased with the pairing, too.

Since Thomas and I were tourists, we asked the girls to choose their pleasure. Without hesitation, they told us that they preferred going to their place instead of to a club or pub. So, we were soon at their apartment, which was less than a mile from the café.

Their "flat" was on the second floor and consisted of one fairly large room with single beds in diagonally opposite corners. Nestled in another corner was a kitchenette with a stove and fridge, while the last corner had a table with four chairs, a record player, and a radio. The center of the room was open and on one side of the kitchenette was a small washroom with a sink and toilet. In spite of the sparse furniture, it was a cozy place to live.

The girls served British ale and we sat around the table drinking, talking, and playing records. Soon Jennifer and I were slow dancing, cheek to cheek as was popular in those days. The feel of her soft body and skin pressed firmly against mine was intoxicating. She smelled faintly of fragrant perfume, which heightened the pleasure of the moment. Thomas and Sarah soon joined us, and to enhance the ambience, we turned off all the lights except for one in the kitchenette area. Occasionally we would stop to change a record, or sit and talk for a few minutes, then resume dancing again.

The music was mostly American records of popular songs or bands—the sweet sounds of romance. Soon we were kissing softly and eventually more intensely. It was obvious that she liked me a lot and I was certainly attracted to her. She asked where we were staying, how long we would be in London, where we had been, and if we could spend more time together. Unfortunately, I explained that we were catching our ship back to the States the next day. She seemed genuinely disappointed and timidly asked if I could spend the night with her instead of going back to the hotel. She said she was sure it would be okay with Sarah. In fact, Sarah had suggested earlier that if Jennifer asked me first, she would ask Thomas, too.

So two lovely girls invited two lonely Yanks to stay over, something no two American girls would ever have done in that day and age.

After the record quit playing, Jennifer turned off the last light and said good night to Sarah and Thomas who, incidentally, were already sitting on Sarah's bed talking. Jennifer took my hand and led me to her bed. She whispered that I should take off as many clothes as I desired, and put them on a bedside chair. I quickly stripped to my briefs and joined her in bed. She had on her bra and panties and after snuggling for a while, we agreed it would be more comfortable to remove everything, which we did.

As we lay together in the nude it felt totally natural. Her skin was as soft and smooth as sweet cream, more so than anyone else I had ever known. What a total delight it was to run my hands over her curves and soft breasts. Of course, I was totally erect and I was sure she would have welcomed my desire to make passionate love. Since neither Thomas nor I had any idea the evening would hold such unexpected pleasures, we hadn't thought to go back to the hotel for rubbers. I could hardly believe I was naked in bed with a gorgeous woman, horny as hell, without protection!

Even though I was not the purist of persons, nor the most honest or trustworthy, the thought of getting such a sweet girl pregnant for my own pleasure was not a viable option.

So without saying a word, I wrapped my body and legs around her silky left thigh, sliding my manhood up and down, slowly at first and soon into a climatic crescendo.

Something then happened that had never happened before in my life. With my head tucked into the nape of her neck and with me softly kissing her, the usual tumescent softening did not occur. I continued to rub against her thigh, much more lubricated than before by my own juices. Soon the tingling and sensitivity returned and I knew the second climax was coming. Although less intense than the first, it was wonderful and I sensed happiness in Jennifer as well. She seemed to feel real pleasure in having aroused me so intensely and, I'm sure, a great deal of relief that she would not have to worry about when or if her next period would occur.

We both then fell into a deep sleep of exhaustion with our bodies entwined in her tiny but snug bed.

All too soon, I felt a push on my shoulder that awakened me from a deep sleep. It was Thomas standing by the bed. It was obviously morning since light was streaming in the only window in the flat. He told me to get up and get dressed, that it was time to catch the morning train back to the continent and Rotterdam. As I looked across the room, I could see Sarah still in bed with her face turned away. I'm not sure why I was relieved, but I guess I didn't want her to see me stark naked. I quickly dressed except for my shirt, Thomas handed me a towel that I assume he got from Sarah, and the two of us rushed down the hall to the floor's common bathroom. Thomas had some soap and some toothpaste (but no toothbrush) so we washed as best we could and brushed our teeth with a dab of toothpaste on a finger.

When we returned to the apartment, the girls were both up, dressed, and smiling brightly. They were fixing toast and jam for breakfast and were brewing American style coffee. We all sat at the table and had a great time talking, eating, and sipping coffee. All too soon, Thomas announced that it was time to catch the train.

I didn't want to leave without getting Jennifer's address and phone number (although I seriously doubted I would ever call) which she wrote on a scratch pad. I gave her my address and told her I would write when I got home. I told how much I had enjoyed meeting her and that I hoped she could come visit me in Oklahoma sometime. While I was quite sincere, I knew it was highly unlikely.

We hugged and kissed our girls, told them goodbye, and hustled back to the hotel. After packing, we caught a taxi and arrived at Victoria Station in plenty of time to catch our 9:05 train. The trip to the coast was rainy, but before noon we were on the ferry headed for the Hook of Holland. We boarded a train to Rotterdam and arrived about 7:30 that evening. While at the station, we ran across two of our friends, Matt and Will, who had been aboard the Zeiterkris earlier that summer, too. The four of us shared a hotel room and found an inexpensive Indonesian restaurant that served a great dinner.

Rotterdam was the most modern city we had encountered in Europe, but there was still some visible damage from extensive bombing during WWII. We briefly toured the city, then headed back to the hotel. As we had throughout our trip, Thomas and I shared a bed and thought nothing of it.

The next morning we went to the pier to find our ship and to our surprise, it was the Zeiterkris. Apparently, Holland-American had switched Harris's trip to a similar student liner, leaving the Zeiterkris to fill our voyage.

After boarding, we received our cabin assignments and discovered they had made an error. Thomas was in a cabin with five other guys, while I shared a cabin with Matt and Will. We tried to get Thomas switched to our cabin, but no one in either cabin was willing to change. Since we spent little time in the cabin anyway, no one really cared.

PART FIVE: THE RETURN

Oh, when the saints go marching in,
Oh, when the saints go marching in,
Lord, I want to be in that number,
When the saints go marching in.

Refrain from
When the Saints Go Marching In,
a popular song performed by many
collegiate singing groups of the '50s.

America!

ince the ship didn't sail until 4:30 that afternoon, Thomas, Will, Matt, and I had plenty of time to get acquainted with the passengers coming aboard. Several of the "shoe" set whom we had met in Europe or on our maiden voyage were onboard. We were excited to see so many familiar faces—besides Will and Matt, we found F.X., Nancy, Betsy, Mary, Sandra, and two sisters, Sue and Priscilla. All of these people were East Coast "aristocracy" and were "shoe" through and through. Although I wasn't truly in their league, I had learned the jargon and ways of the "elite" and managed to fit in as if I had always been a Yankee blueblood.

With our gang of five guys and six gals established, we spent the better part of the return voyage together. Although we were not intentionally being snobbish, for the most part we ignored the rest of the passengers and crew. While we would smile and be friendly to the others, we never included them in our activities. Whether sunning on the deck or congregating at the bar, it was only our group. We built our own little world and chose not to invite anyone else.

The return trip was, nevertheless, very boring. The enthusiasm of the first sailing was gone. Everyone was ready to resume his or her American life. The things we enjoyed the most on the first voyage, like the student led talent shows and activities, never occurred. To add insult to injury, skirting a major storm delayed our arrival an extra day.

We did sunbathe in the afternoons when the weather allowed (perhaps half of the time), hit the nightclub-bar in the evening, and had one "vino" party. Although the girls were reasonably cute, there was no romance: it was as if we were all so "cool" that such activity would be too plebeian and gauche. We were just friends hanging out together, joking, laughing, and making small talk. Nothing serious was going on, which was the comfortable, natural way we wanted it to be—friends, nothing more.

With so few distractions to interrupt my thoughts, I had a great deal of time to reflect on the past two years of my life—both the good and the bad.

My love affair with Norma had been a great learning experience since it was the first time I had serious regular sex with a girlfriend. I must admit, it was a hell of a lot better than just making out, even if the latter resulted in an occasional orgasm. I never felt a true, deep commitment to Norma, nor did I get the impression that she was deeply in love with me. I do believe that if we had still been together at graduation, she would have married me if I had popped the question. I'm certain such a marriage would have been a mistake, most likely one that ended in divorce.

I honestly believe that two people must be totally in love and share the bond many refer to as "chemistry," in order to survive both the good and bad things that happen in a marriage. If Norma had truly loved me, I believe she would have done everything in her power to win me back on our last weekend together. Instead, she was cold and indifferent. I believe that if true love exists, anyone would jump at a second chance if given the opportunity. This may or may not be true, but it made perfect sense while basking in the sunlight on the ship's deck.

My thoughts of Marian were wonderfully bitter-sweet. I felt lucky to have met such a great girl, even though it ended in total frustration. Never had the old adage, "'Tis better to have loved and lost than never to have loved at all," been more true. The chemistry between us was unmistakable, and I can only imagine what it could have been like if allowed to fully mature and blossom.

There was no doubt in my mind that if we had met earlier in our lives we would have had a deep, serious love affair. It was easy to imagine a happy marriage with Marian, one that could survive all the rough spots in its path. Of course, we'll never know if it could have occurred, but in my heart I'm certain that it would.

Aside from love and marriage, I felt I learned a great deal from the girls in Holland, France, and even Italy. The ability to enjoy sex without emotional ties was very clear. The mechanical act of sex with a highly skilled artisan like the French girl was quite wonderful and the friendly Dutch girl was memorable as well. The indifference of the Italian woman definitely took the spark out of the act. While I suppose it was better than nothing, I doubt that it was worth the hassle. In hindsight, the lesson was simple: unless a girl is excited and eager, don't waste your money. In fact, sex that is freely given is much more satisfying.

Last, I thought of the lovely English girl, Jennifer. Had I met her first, I might not have left London to tour Europe at all. In the least, I would have made frequent returns to England after short trips to the continent, which would have hindered my plans with Thomas and Harris. Although I would probably have chosen to go with them and visit Jennifer at the end of our adventure, it would have been a difficult choice.

I suppose things work out for the best. I hoped that after I returned home and my life settled down, she could come for a visit. It would be so nice to see her again and really get to know her. She was definitely not "shoe," not socially elite, which made me wonder if she could be a suitable wife. Looking back, it was a stupid thought, yet it seemed very real at the time. How wrong I was—but that is another story.

I also had the chance to reflect on post-WWII Europe. The Germans definitely had a superiority complex, clearly expressed by their eager work ethic and industrial ability. Driven by the schizophrenic Hitler, they goose-stepped their way through Europe imposing their will on docile France, Belgium, Holland, Poland and the Balkans. Had Hitler stopped at the borders of continental Europe, the French would probably be speaking German to this day. However, by invading Russia and taking on the "bulldog" Great Britain, he sealed his fate. Even if there had been no "Pearl Harbor," the USA would have come to the aid of England and Churchill, which would have been the final nail in Hitler's coffin.

With Germany destroyed, the rest of Europe fell back to the lazy, carefree lifestyles that we experienced in the Low Countries, France, and Italy. While the Germans were rebuilding, there was no sense of any ulterior motive—it just seemed to be their nature. They like to eat wurst, drink beer, and work their asses off. When you think about it, Americans are quite similar. Plenty of us like to eat hot dogs, drink cokes or beer, and work our asses off.

One final thought about Europe. The abundance of architectural marvels, fantastic works of art and sculpture, and historical ruins, were certainly more than one could see or comprehend in a lifetime, much less in one short summer. Nevertheless, the three of us busted our butts to see, hear, and absorb all the wonderful sights and sounds of mid-twentieth century Europe. It truly was the adventure of a lifetime, well worth every ounce of scheming and hard work necessary to make it a reality. I truly believe that Thomas and Harris shared a similar emotional enrichment, and I know we will carry the treasured memories in our souls for the rest of our lives.

As my saga of the early '50s nears its end, I hope my tales have been enlightening. While no great mysteries were solved, no dangerous escapes survived, and no great treasures were found, three young men became infinitely wiser to the ways of the world and electrified about the possibilities life held.

As New York harbor and the Statue of Liberty grew closer, I imagined the excitement immigrants must experience coming to this great land. Although I was just an American citizen returning home, the moment was stirring.

Thomas's parents were waiting at the pier and

after hugs and handshakes, we loaded the luggage and headed for Grand Central Station. An afternoon train was leaving for St. Louis, where I could transfer to the Santa Fe. In a short time, I would be back in Oklahoma City. Over lunch Thomas and I went on and on about our great adventures, omitting the details about the girls, of course. Thomas's parents were obviously pleased that their money had been well spent. My parents reacted the same way as I eagerly described my trip.

One of the first things I did after returning was to write Thomas's parents to thank them for helping me in NYC and letting me stay in their home the night before we left for Europe. I wished Thomas all the best for his junior year at Yale and hoped he made the starting fullback position on the varsity football team. I received a nice reply, expressing how much they enjoyed having me and that they hoped I did well in Med school. Since Thomas and I both became busy with academic endeavors, that was the last contact we shared.

I also wrote two letters to Jennifer, and her replies were both very sweet. Unfortunately, the stress and demands of my new mistress—medicine— extinguished the spark of our relationship by plunging me into a new and demanding adventure. Perhaps, some day, there will be a sequel titled, *Class of '58: Memoirs of a Med Student.* If you enjoyed this book, please let the Publisher know—the story of the next four years will surprise you!

Afterword

In the foreword, I mentioned the pitfalls of writing memoirs. I alluded to the necessary deviation from fact in order to relate the stories in a way that would convey the essence of the times.

The tales I have written are basically true, although not necessarily with the person designated. I resurrected my European adventure from a diary I kept that summer and the rest from vivid memories. Since the time I was two years old, I have always had the ability to recall events. I remember my childhood, my school chums (and most of their names) as well as the names of all my elementary and high school teachers. This ability is, of course, a genetic gift, which I am grateful to have received.

I hope you found my story both engaging and entertaining, and that it provided a glimpse into a special time in history. I enjoyed writing it almost as much as I enjoyed living it!

Dr. David William Foerster